HAL•LEONARD

INSTRUMENTAL
PLAY-ALONG

AUDIO
ACCESS
INCLUDED

PLAYBACK+
Speed • Pitch • Balance • Loop

ALTO SAX

FAVORITE Disney SONGS

T0066215

Audio arrangements by Peter Deneff

To access audio, visit:
www.halleonard.com/mylibrary

Enter Code
3967-2325-9050-4434

ISBN 978-1-70514-270-7

Visit Hal Leonard Online at
www.halleonard.com

Contact us:
Hal Leonard
7777 West Bluemound Road
Milwaukee, WI 53213
Email: info@halleonard.com

In Europe, contact:
Hal Leonard Europe Limited
42 Wigmore Street
Marylebone, London, W1U 2RN
Email: info@halleonardeurope.com

In Australia, contact:
Hal Leonard Australia Pty. Ltd.
4 Lentara Court
Cheltenham, Victoria, 3192 Australia
Email: info@halleonard.com.au

CONTENTS

THE BALLAD OF THE LONESOME COWBOY

from TOY STORY 4

ALTO SAX

Music and Lyrics by
RANDY NEWMAN

EVERMORE
from BEAUTY AND THE BEAST

ALTO SAX

Music by ALAN MENKEN
Lyrics by TIM RICE

HOW DOES A MOMENT LAST FOREVER

from BEAUTY AND THE BEAST

ALTO SAX

Music by ALAN MENKEN
Lyrics by TIM RICE

HOW FAR I'LL GO
from MOANA

ALTO SAX

Music and Lyrics by
LIN-MANUEL MIRANDA

Moderately
Guitar

INTO THE UNKNOWN
from FROZEN 2

ALTO SAX

Music and Lyrics by KRISTEN ANDERSON-LOPEZ
and ROBERT LOPEZ

9

IT'S ALL RIGHT

featured in SOUL

ALTO SAX

Words and Music by
CURTIS MAYFIELD

LAVA
from LAVA

ALTO SAX

Music and Lyrics by
JAMES FORD MURPHY

LEAD THE WAY

from RAYA AND THE LAST DRAGON

ALTO SAX

Music and Lyrics by
JHENÉ AIKO

THE PLACE WHERE LOST THINGS GO

from MARY POPPINS RETURNS

ALTO SAX

Music by MARC SHAIMAN
Lyrics by SCOTT WITTMAN and MARC SHAIMAN

NEVER TOO LATE

from THE LION KING 2019

ALTO SAX

Music by ELTON JOHN
Lyrics by TIM RICE

SPEECHLESS
from ALADDIN (2019)

ALTO SAX

Music by ALAN MENKEN
Lyrics by BENJ PASEK
and JUSTIN PAUL

Moderately

TOUCH THE SKY

from BRAVE

ALTO SAX

Music by ALEXANDER L. MANDEL
Lyrics by ALEXANDER L. MANDEL
and MARK ANDREWS

TRY EVERYTHING
from ZOOTOPIA

ALTO SAX

Words and Music by SIA FURLER,
TOR ERIK HERMANSEN and MIKKEL ERIKSEN

YOU'RE WELCOME

from MOANA

ALTO SAX

Music and Lyrics by
LIN-MANUEL MIRANDA

REMEMBER ME
(Ernesto de la Cruz)
from COCO

ALTO SAX

Words and Music by KRISTEN ANDERSON-LOPEZ
and ROBERT LOPEZ